Bowmar/Noble Handwriting H

Reviewers

Sister Andrew Maureen, I. H. M.
Principal
Somerdale, New Jersey

Dr. Fred Chavez
Specialist, Elementary Reading
Los Angeles, California

Beverly Ellis
Elementary Language Arts Supervisor
Springfield, Missouri

Otis H. Lovelace, Jr.
Principal
Charlotte County, Virginia

Dr. Philip Mann
Professor of Psychology
University of Miami, Florida

Dr. Virginia S. Melton
College of Education
Louisiana Tech University, Louisiana

Jeannie Russell
Instructional Specialist
Rosemead, California

Sister Kathleen T. Sullivan
District Superintendent
Staten Island, New York

Mary Janet Taylor
Director of Elementary Instruction
Blytheville, Arkansas

Sister Mary Theiss
Curriculum Coordinator
Milwaukee, Wisconsin

I0798645

McGraw-Hill School Division
1200 Northwest 63rd Street
Oklahoma City, Oklahoma 73116-5712

Cover Illustration: Mike Wimmer
Illustrations: Clovis Martin

ISBN 0-07-375768-3
ISBN 0-8372-4075-1

31 LKV 25

PRE-TEST

Read, and the storyteller seems to sit at your elbow. Aesop, Homer, Virgil, and Xenophon tell you ancient tales. You feel as though you are taking part in the exciting adventure stories of Washington Irving, James Fenimore Cooper, Herman Melville, and Zane Grey. Quietly, the books of Ezra Jack Keats, P. L. Travers, Ursula Nordstrom, E. B. White, and Scott O'Dell speak to you. There is nothing to equal the joy of reading a good story.

Directions: Copy the paragraph.

www.ingramcontent.com/pod-product-compliance
Lightning Source LLC
LaVergne TN
LVHW071131190826
846010LV00028B/104

* 9 7 8 0 6 1 5 1 5 1 8 4 7 *

CURSIVE ALPHABET

Models of all the cursive letters and numerals are presented on this page.

Aa Bb Cc Dd Ee

Ff Gg Hh Ii Jj

Kk Ll Mm Nn Oo

Pp Qq Rr Ss Tt

Uu Vv Ww Xx Yy Zz

1 2 3 4 5 6 7 8 9 10

Directions: Copy the letters and numerals.

a

IMPROVING HANDWRITING: WATCH-OUT LETTERS

WATCH OUT

The oval in small **a** should be closed at the top. The end stroke of small **a** should touch the baseline.

a a a aaaaa alfalfa area

auto audience auditorium aunt

acid association accident account

aorta abandon almanac algebra

Anita had a leading part in a play.

The audience applauded her acting.

Directions: Copy the letters, words, and sentences.

b

IMPROVING HANDWRITING: WATCH-OUT LETTERS

WATCH OUT

The end stroke of small **b** should be kept close to the guideline.

b b b bbbbb bubbles bulb

blink belief blizzard blister

beginning ballot business boost

barbecue bribe bamboo bobsled

Robby read a biography of Babe Ruth.

Babe Ruth had great batting ability.

Directions: Copy the letters, words, and sentences.

d

IMPROVING HANDWRITING: WATCH-OUT LETTERS

WATCH OUT

The oval of small **d** should be closed at the stem. Small **d** is two-thirds of a space high.

1 2 d dddddd did demand

decline declare declaration closed

dreadful defeated depend dodge

dared dividend dogwood discarded

The debate was held in the auditorium.

Each debator defended one position.

Directions: Copy the letters, words, and sentences.

IMPROVING HANDWRITING: WATCH-OUT LETTERS

e

WATCH OUT

The top of small **e** should be rounded and the loop should be open.

e eeee extreme effect

eighty experience science their

eve example electrical engage

eagle esteem elevate exceed

Eileen exercises every day at seven.

She eats a healthy breakfast at eight.

Directions: Copy the letters, words, and sentences.

h

IMPROVING HANDWRITING: WATCH-OUT LETTERS

WATCH OUT

The hill in small **h** should be well rounded. The second stroke of small **h** should curve up in a small, well-rounded hill.

1 2 h h hhhhh high height

halibut holiday helium highlight

hush healthy hillside hatchet

hunch heather hopscotch hyacinth

Watch the helicopter hover in the sky.

The helicopter has a huge propeller.

Directions: Copy the letters, words, and sentences.

i

IMPROVING HANDWRITING: WATCH-OUT LETTERS

WATCH OUT

The top of small **i** should be pointed and closed. Small **i** should be dotted after all the letters in a word are written.

i i dot i iiiii incline ignite

intelligent identified impatient

instruction investigation imagine

illegible identification irritation

I will write the invitations tonight.

Akemi will mail them in the morning.

Directions: Copy the letters, words, and sentences.

USING HANDWRITING: PARAGRAPH

The title of this paragraph is centered on the first line with a blank line below. The first line of a paragraph is always indented with a space as wide as a capital **O.**

The Sahara

The Sahara, which extends across northern Africa, is the world's largest desert. Although parts of the Sahara have the huge sand dunes that we associate with deserts, most of the Sahara consists of rocky plateaus and pebbled plains. Rainfall averages only about eight inches per year. Less than two million people live in the Sahara.

 Directions: Copy the paragraph.

USING HANDWRITING: POEM

Every other line of this poem is indented and the first word of each line is capitalized.

Learning to Write

No matter how you strive to write
  With pens and quarts of ink,
You'll never learn to do it right
  Unless you learn to think.

To stop awhile and plan with care
  Will help you write with ease;
The time you take to well prepare
  Will make your writing please.

Directions: Copy the poem.

CONNECTIVES

Connectives join letters together to form words. Connectives also determine the spacing between letters in words.

Under-curve connectives

assure merit kettle crisis

resist sleet tissue distress

Over-curve connectives

hand exam cacao mammal

many caddy mango sandy

Long under-curve and long over-curve connectives

genius juggle yeast zeal

gallop journal yam zone

 Directions: Copy the words.

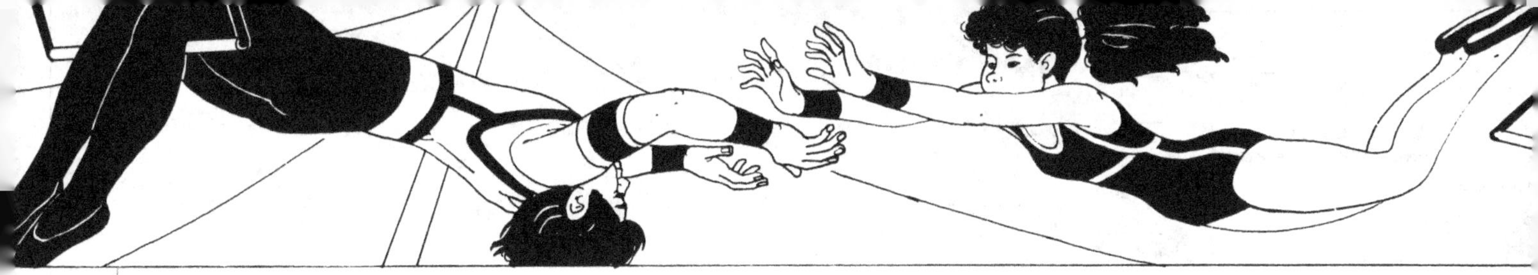

Connectives from the baseline

flame *popular* *quaint* *fresh*

quill *paragraph* *fault* *peril*

Bridge connectives

basis *occur* *vocal* *walnut*

body *oasis* *vault* *wooden*

Horizontal connectives

bright *object* *vivid* *whole*

believe *orbit* *version* *weave*

Directions: Copy the words.

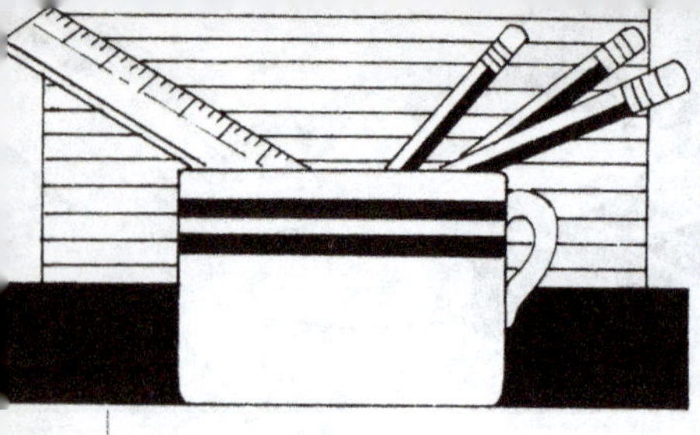

IMPROVING HANDWRITING: SIZE

Checking your letters for size will help you to improve your handwriting. Lines drawn with a ruler should just touch the tops of your letters at three different heights.

Wrong

This writing is too large.

Wrong

This writing is too small.

Right

This handwriting is just right.

Right

These letters are the right heights.

 Directions: Copy the correct sentences. Use a ruler as you check for size.

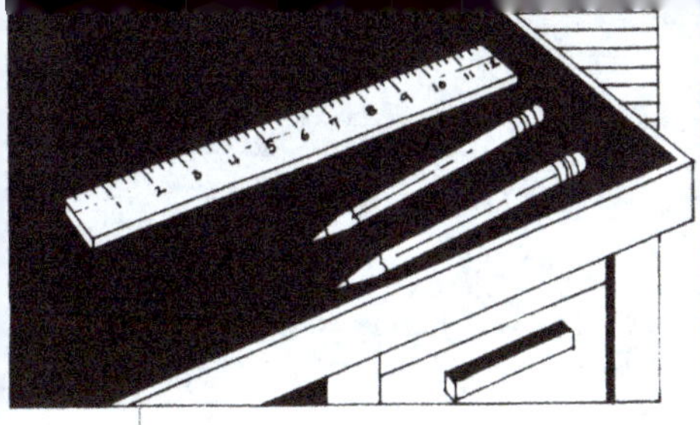

IMPROVING HANDWRITING: SLANT

Checking your letters for slant will help you to improve your handwriting. Dashed lines drawn through the downstrokes of your letters should be parallel and slanted.

Wrong

This writing slants too far forward.

Wrong

This writing slants in all directions.

Right

This writing is slanted correctly.

Right

Keep your downstrokes parallel.

Directions: Copy the correct sentences. Use a ruler as you check for slant.

USING HANDWRITING: EDITORIAL

An editorial usually contains one or more paragraphs. The hyphens in this editorial are used to separate the two parts of a compound word. Hyphens are made just below the guideline.

Time for a Clean-Up!

Everyone is against pollution. Everyone wants to live in a clean environment. But, lately, we've noticed that our school environment is not as neat or clean as it could be. The school grounds are messy and dirty. They are covered with pieces of paper, scraps of food, and other unsightly litter. The grounds have been polluted by our carelessness.

Let's all pitch in and pick up the trash! The teachers have agreed to help us. Let's meet tomorrow at noon in front of the cafeteria. Working together, we can clean up the mess quickly and easily. Then, if each of us remembers to pick up after herself or himself every day, the school grounds will stay sparkling clean.

Don't you agree that it's time for a clean-up! Show your support tomorrow at noon!

 Directions: Copy the editorial.

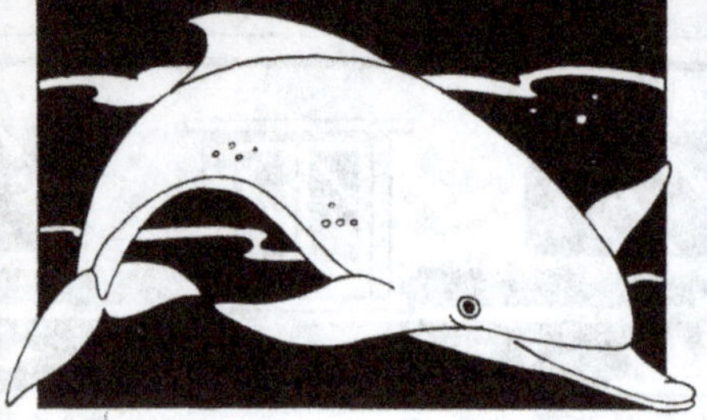

PROGRESS PAGES

The scarlet blossoms of an azalea shrub are shaped like a trumpet.

The waxy flowers of a begonia plant vary in color from pink to red.

The showy blossoms of the hydrangea shrub may be white, pink, or bluish.

The colorful flowers of an iris plant range through all colors of a rainbow.

Directions: Copy the sentences.

A deciduous tree sheds its leaves every year and then grows new ones.

The chestnut, a deciduous tree, is valued for its durable wood and edible nuts.

The leaves of an evergreen tree remain green throughout the entire year.

The cedar, an evergreen tree, has a sweet, fresh aroma and tough, reddish wood.

Directions: Copy the sentences.

MANUSCRIPT ALPHABET

Manuscript writing is useful in preparing posters, labels, signs, greeting cards, forms, charts, and tables.

Aa Bb Cc Dd Ee Ff Gg

Hh Ii Jj Kk Ll Mm Nn Oo

Pp Qq Rr Ss Tt Uu Vv Ww

Xx Yy Zz 1 2 3 4 5 6 7 8 9 10

Auditorium Library Cafeteria

History Biology Pre-Algebra

 Directions: Copy the letters, numerals, and words.

USING HANDWRITING: FORMS

Manuscript writing is often used to fill out forms, such as the catalog order form below.

CATALOG ORDER D467

NAME: Carmen Delgado

ADDRESS: 3547 June St.

Denver, CO 80236

PHONE: (303) 975-6845

ITEM NAME: Solar-Powered Calculator

ITEM NUMBER: 2576 N QUANTITY: 1

PRICE: $10.98

TAX: .66

SHIPPING CHARGE: 2.25

TOTAL CHARGE: $13.89

CATALOG ORDER D467

NAME:

ADDRESS:

PHONE:

ITEM NAME:

ITEM NUMBER: QUANTITY:

PRICE:

TAX:

SHIPPING CHARGE:

TOTAL CHARGE:

Directions: Copy the catalog order form.

m

IMPROVING HANDWRITING: WATCH-OUT LETTERS

WATCH OUT

The three hills in small **m** should be well rounded. All the hills in small **m** should be the same height.

1 2 3 m mmmmmm minimum

mowing meadow minnow marrow

memory maximum member mammal

mimic membrane microfilm medium

American minnows are small fish.

Common minnows are 15 centimeters long.

 Directions: Copy the letters, words, and sentences.

n

IMPROVING HANDWRITING: WATCH-OUT LETTERS

WATCH OUT

The two hills in small **n** should be well rounded. Both hills in small **n** should be the same height.

n n n nnnnnn nine noon

numb union nuance unknown

neon notion nineteen nonsense

nylon ninth nitrogen notation

Our nation is a union of states.

Washington, D.C., is our nation's capital.

Directions: Copy the letters, words, and sentences.

o

IMPROVING HANDWRITING: WATCH-OUT LETTERS

WATCH OUT

The end stroke of small **o** should be close to the guideline. The oval in small **o** should be closed.

o o o ooooo oppose overtook

oak accompany apology oath

ounce ocean once office

offshore overdo outcome onlooker

The divers explored the ocean floor.

They saw colorful coral formations.

Directions: Copy the letters, words, and sentences.

r

IMPROVING HANDWRITING: WATCH-OUT LETTERS

WATCH OUT

The top of small **r** should be slanted. Small **r** has a small point that should extend a little above the guideline.

r r r r rrrrr refer rare

require rider retire rigorous

rowers rural robbery radiator

rudder rotor radar raspberry

Your history report is due on Friday.

Do your research in the library.

Directions: Copy the letters, words, and sentences.

t

IMPROVING HANDWRITING: WATCH-OUT LETTERS

WATCH OUT

The stem of small **t** should be closed. Small **t** should be crossed after all the letters in a word are written. Small **t** is two-thirds of a space high.

1 2 across t tttt text tooth

talent title trouble tilted

tomato treaty total tourist

tenant thrifty tutor trotted

What time does the tour start?

It starts exactly at eight tonight.

 Directions: Copy the letters, words, and sentences.

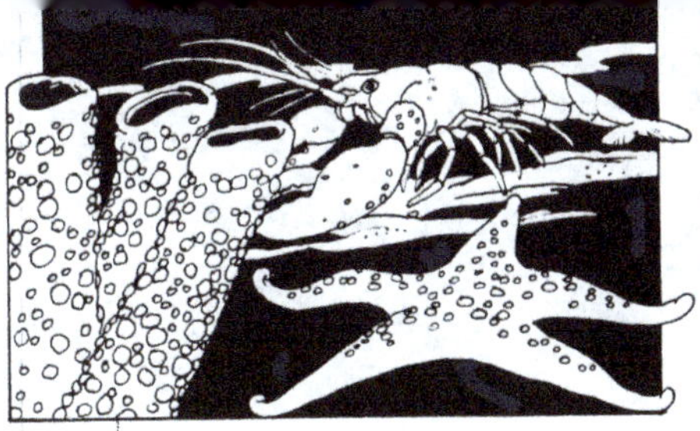

USING HANDWRITING: PARAGRAPH

This paragraph, which is written in manuscript letters, contains all the watch-out letters.

The ocean floor is covered with spiny animals, such as sea urchins and starfish. Animals with heavy shells, such as lobsters and crabs, also live at the bottom of the sea. These animals are free to walk or swim through the deep waters as they search for food. Other animals, such as oysters, corals, and sponges, however, are attached to the ocean floor and stay in one position on the ocean bottom all of their lives.

Directions: Copy the paragraph using cursive handwriting.

USING HANDWRITING: DIARY ENTRY

In this diary, the date of the entry is written in the upper right corner. A blank line follows the date.

April 16, 1987

Today I traveled more than 200 years into the past. No, I didn't use a time machine. And no, I didn't have a dream. Today, I visited colonial Williamsburg in Virginia. There, the past is frozen in time. I was no longer living in the present. Instead, I was whisked back to the 1700's, to colonial times, when our nation was young.

What did I do and see during my journey into the past? I rode in a horse-drawn carriage. I chatted with guides dressed in colonial costumes. I admired skills of artisans who dipped candles, hammered horseshoes, wove cloth, carved cabinets, and fashioned fancy wigs. And I wondered what it would have been like to have lived then, without cars, TV's, electricity, or telephones. What do you think?

 Directions: Copy the diary entry.

WATCH OUT

IMPROVING HANDWRITING: WATCH-OUT NUMERALS

WATCH OUT

Be careful: **5's** can look like **3's**
6's can look like **0's**
7's can look like **1's**

Start the last stroke of **5** where you began the numeral.

5 5 5 55555 55555 55555

Keep the loop in **6** between the guideline and the baseline.

6 6 66666 66666 66666

Keep the downstroke of **7** straight and slanted to the left.

7 7 7 77777 77777 77777

Find the average of 57, 65, and 76.

Is 66 the correct answer?

 Directions: Copy the numerals and sentences.

USING HANDWRITING: PARAGRAPH

This paragraph contains the watch-out numerals: **5, 6, and 7.**

How high is the highest moutain? Mount Everest, the world's highest mountain, rises 29,028 feet. Mount Cotopaxi in the Andes, the highest active volcano in the world, is 19,347 feet high. Mauna Kea, a volcano in Hawaii, is the world's highest island peak, rising 13,796 feet. Mauna Loa, another volcanic peak in Hawaii, rises 13,677 feet. Lassen Peak in California, an active volcano on the United States mainland, rises 10,457 feet above sea level.

Directions: Copy the paragraph.

USING HANDWRITING: BUDGET

The numerals in this budget are lined up in columns. The decimal points in each column are placed one under the other.

My Budget for the Week Ending March 20

		Income	Expenses
14	Mon.		
	Cash on hand	$ 3.00	
	Allowance	$ 5.50	
15	Tues.		
	Notebook		$ .50
16	Wed.		
	Cleaning yard	$ 5.50	
17	Thurs.		
	No expenses		
18	Fri.		
	Pen		$ 1.00
19	Sat.		
	Movies		$ 11.00
20	Sun.		
	Soccer game		$ 1.00
	Totals	$14.00	$ 13.50
	Cash on hand	$ .50	

Directions: Copy the budget.

USING HANDWRITING: COMPOSITION

Sets of quotation marks are used in this composition to set off a short title and a nickname. Quotation marks are shaped like commas.

"Old Ironsides"

"Old Ironsides" is the popular name for the Constitution, a famous battleship of the United States Navy. The ship earned its nickname in the War of 1812 when a sailor is said to have seen ammunition from the British guns bouncing off the wooden sides of the ship. He cried aloud that the ship's sides seemed to be made of iron.

After many victorious battles, the Constitution was declared unseaworthy in 1830. But public interest in the ship became so strong that it was rebuilt three times. In 1934, "Old Ironsides" found a permanent home in Boston, where it is docked on the Charles River. There, "Old Ironsides," the oldest warship in the world that is still afloat, is viewed by thousands of visitors each year.

Directions: Copy the composition.

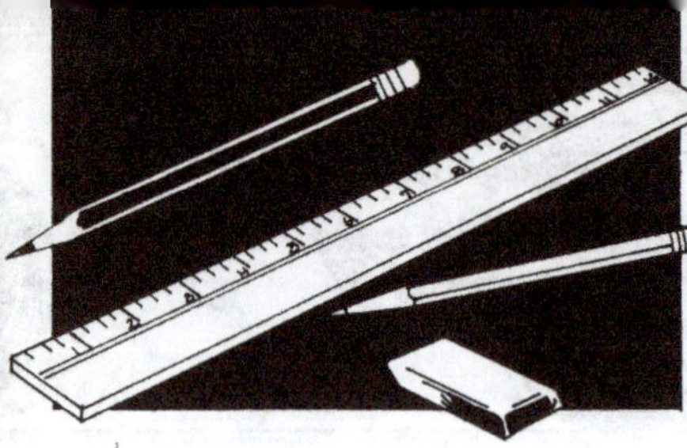

IMPROVING HANDWRITING: SPACING WORDS

Checking the spacing between words will help you to improve your handwriting. The space between words should be as wide as a small **o.**

Wrong

This spacing is too wide.

Wrong

This spacing is too close and crowded.

Right

This spacing is just right.

Right

Keep the width of an o between words.

Directions: Copy the correct sentences. Use a ruler as you check for spacing between words.

IMPROVING HANDWRITING: SPACING LETTERS

Checking the spacing between letters in words will help you to improve your handwriting. Your spacing should be compared to correctly formed models.

Wrong

This spacing is too wide.

Wrong

This spacing is too narrow.

Right

This spacing is just right.

Right

Leave uniform spacing between letters.

Directions: Copy the correct sentences and check your letters for spacing.

USING HANDWRITING: OUTLINE

The main topics in an outline start with roman numerals, the subtopics begin with capital letters, and the details begin with arabic numerals. All subtopics and details are indented.

Mexico

I. History
  A. Great Indian civilizations
    1. The Mayas
    2. The Aztecs
  B. Spanish rule and influence

II. Modern life
  A. Life in large cities
  B. Life in small villages

III. Natural resources
  A. Rich farmland
    1. Fertile soil
    2. Sufficient rainfall
  B. Rich mineral deposits
    1. Gold and silver
    2. Coal and copper
    3. Petroleum and natural gas
  C. Thick forests
    1. Hard woods for furniture
    2. Soft woods for pulp and paper

 Directions: Copy the outline.

PROGRESS PAGES

A manatee, or sea cow, is a clumsy mammal that lives in warm waters.

A fully grown manatee weighs about 1500 pounds, or 680 kilograms.

A narwhal, a small whale, swims in arctic waters; a male narwhal has a tusk.

Not including its tusk, a male narwhal is about 15 feet, or 5 meters, long.

Directions: Copy the sentences.

The tuna, a large saltwater fish, lives in temperate and tropical water zones.

The tuna, a fast swimmer, can swim up to 45 miles, or 72 kilometers, per hour.

A sting ray, a large, flat fish, uses its to inflict a painful, poisonous wound.

Not including its tail, a sting ray grows to be about 7 feet, or 2 meters, long.

Directions: Copy the sentences.

USING HANDWRITING: POSTER

Manuscript writing is often used on posters. This poster is written on unlined paper, and each line of the poster is centered.

VOTE! VOTE! VOTE! VOTE!

ELECTION NEWS

Student Council elections
will be held on
Tuesday, November 15,
in the library.

The nominees for
Student Council President are:
Jenny Mckee
Blanca Romero
Mark Zimmerman.

DON'T FORGET TO VOTE!

YOUR VOTE CAN MAKE A DIFFERENCE!

VOTE! VOTE! VOTE! VOTE!

Directions: Copy the poster using manuscript handwriting.

SMALL LETTERS

All of the small letters, except the watch-out letters, are presented on these two pages.

f f f fortify offer

g g g gadget geology

j j j j juggle injury

p p p p peppy pulp

q q q q quiz inquiry

y y y yearly z z z fuzzy

 Directions: Copy the letters and words.

c cancel critic

k knuckle knack

l label liable

s subside sparse

u untrue v valve

w widow slant across x exile

Directions: Copy the letters and words.

CAPITAL LETTERS

Capital **A, B, C, E, G, H, J,** and **K** are always joined to the next letter in a word. Capital **D, F, I,** and **L** are not joined to the next letter.

A A Argentina August

B B Baltimore Boston

C C Chinese Canadian

D D D Doris Diana

E E Eskimo Eurasia

F F F F Fiji Friday

 Directions: Copy the letters and words.

G G G G G Glasgow Georgia

H H H H H Halifax Helsinki

I I I I Iberia India

J J J Julio January

K K K K K Korea Kenji

L L L L London Liverpool

Directions: Copy the letters and words.

CAPITAL LETTERS

Capital **M, N, R, S, U, Y,** and **Z** are always joined to the next letter in a word. Capital **O, P, Q, T, V, W,** and **X** are not joined to the next letter.

M M M Madrid Mediterranean

N N Navajo November

O O O Oceania Olivia

P P P Pandora Polaris

Q Q Q Quito Quebec

R R R Rockies Rembrandt

 Directions: Copy the letters and words.

S S Senegal Sweden

T T Thien Topeka

U U Ursula V Vienna

W W Wisconsin Welsh

X X Xenia Xenophon

Y Y Yolanda Z Z Zaire

Directions: Copy the letters and words.

MATH PROBLEMS WITH FRACTIONS

In math problems, the numerals are often lined up in columns and rows. The numerals in fractions are a little less than one-third of a space high.

$$3\tfrac{1}{6} + 4\tfrac{1}{6} = 7\tfrac{2}{6} = 7\tfrac{1}{3}$$

$$2\tfrac{1}{8} + 6\tfrac{3}{8} = \quad$$

$$7\tfrac{5}{12} + 5\tfrac{3}{12} = \quad$$

$$11\tfrac{3}{4} - 5\tfrac{1}{4} = 6\tfrac{2}{4} = 6\tfrac{1}{2}$$

$$10\tfrac{11}{16} - 4\tfrac{3}{16} = \quad$$

$$9\tfrac{7}{10} - 6\tfrac{2}{10} = \quad$$

$$\tfrac{2}{3} \times \tfrac{3}{4} = \tfrac{6}{12} = \tfrac{1}{2}$$

$$\tfrac{1}{2} \times \tfrac{2}{7} = \quad = \quad$$

$$\tfrac{1}{6} \times \tfrac{2}{3} = \tfrac{2}{18} = \tfrac{1}{9}$$

$$\tfrac{6}{8} \times \tfrac{2}{3} = \quad = \quad$$

Directions: Copy and solve the problems.

USING HANDWRITING: MATH PROBLEMS

A mixed number contains a whole number and a fraction. Numerals for whole numbers are two-thirds of a space high. Numerals in fractions are a little less than one-third of a space high.

Tricia worked $3\frac{1}{4}$ hours after school on Monday, $4\frac{1}{4}$ hours on Tuesday, and $5\frac{1}{4}$ hours on Friday. How many hours did she work in all?

$$3\tfrac{1}{4} + 4\tfrac{1}{4} + 5\tfrac{1}{4} = 12\tfrac{3}{4}$$

Tricia worked __ hours.

Last weekend Alex worked in a supermarket for $7\frac{1}{2}$ hours. He earned \$4 an hour. How much money did Alex earn?

$$7\tfrac{1}{2} \times 4 = \tfrac{15}{2} \times \tfrac{4}{1} = \tfrac{60}{2} = 30$$

Alex earned ____ dollars.

Directions: Copy and solve the problems.

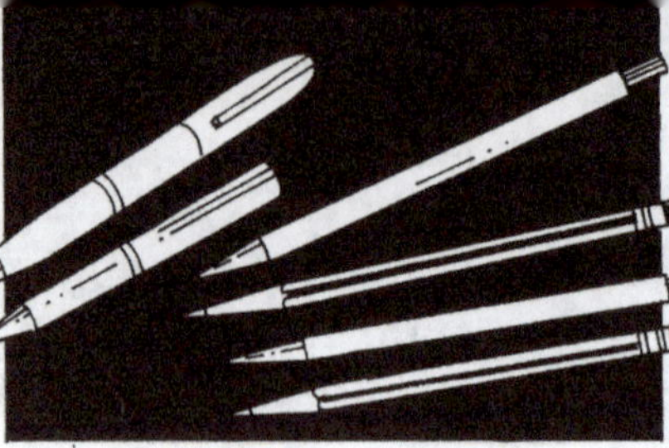

IMPROVING HANDWRITING: SHAPE

Checking your letters for shape by comparing them to correctly formed models will help you to improve your handwriting.

Wrong

These letters are too wide.

Wrong

These letters are too narrow.

Right

These letters are the right shape.

Right

Compare your letters with the models.

 Directions: Copy the correct sentences and check your letters for shape.

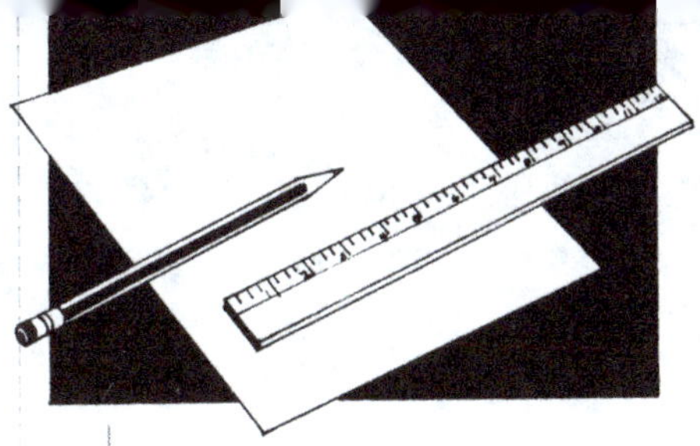

IMPROVING HANDWRITING: ALIGNMENT

Checking the alignment of your letters will help you to improve your handwriting. All your letters should sit on a straight line drawn through the bases of your letters.

Wrong

These letters are above the baseline.

Wrong

This is above and below the baseline.

Right

These letters are written correctly.

Right

Every letter must sit on the baseline.

Directions: Copy the correct sentences. Use a ruler as you check for alignment.

USING HANDWRITING: BIOGRAPHY

The hyphens in this biography are used to separate parts of words that do not fit on the line, as well as the two parts of compound words. Hyphens are made just below the guideline.

Sally Ride

Sally Kristen Ride, astronaut and
physicist, was born in 1951 in
Los Angeles, California. As a young
girl, she was a gifted athlete and
student. After graduating from Stan-
ford University in 1978 with a Ph.D.
in physics, Sally Ride entered the
astronaut program.

The United States sent its first
satellite into orbit around the Earth
in 1958. Twenty-five years later,
in 1983, during a six-day, space-
shuttle flight, astronaut Sally Ride
became the first American woman
to travel in space. As a mission
specialist aboard the space shuttle,
Sally Ride, along with her fellow
astronauts, carried out many scien-
tific experiments that helped increase
our knowledge and understanding of
the frontier of space.

Directions: Copy the biography.

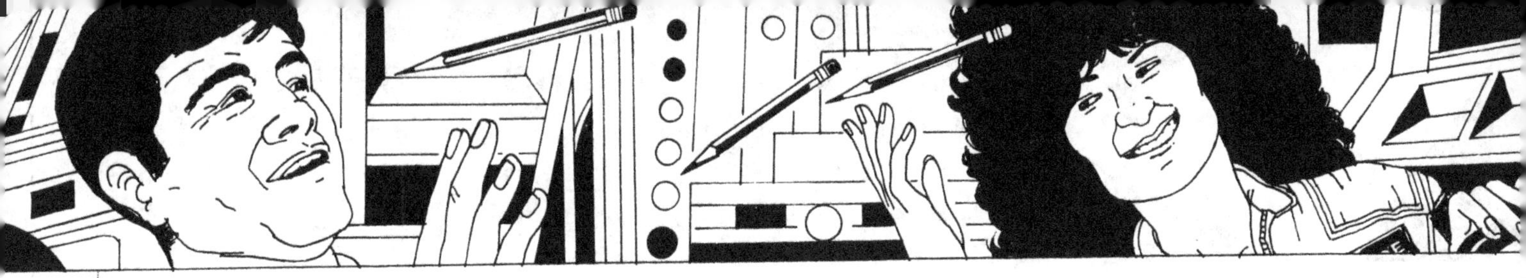

IMPROVING HANDWRITING: OVERALL APPEARANCE

Checking the overall appearance of your written work will help you to improve your handwriting. A paper should have even margins and neat handwriting.

(Use Your Name) (Use Today's Date)

Thomas Alva Edison

Thomas Alva Edison was probably the greatest inventor who ever lived. During his life, Edison invented more than 1000 useful things. The electric light was his greatest invention. Edison made electric lights available to millions by designing the world's first electric power station.

Edison set up his first laboratory in the basement of his home in 1857, when he was ten years old. He worked on his inventions night and day. Once, when he made more than 10,000 unsuccess-ful experiments on a storage battery, the undaunted inventor exclaimed, "I have not failed. I've just found 10,000 ways that won't work."

By the time he died in 1931, Thomas Edison, the "wizard of Menlo Park," was well-loved and admired.

Directions: Copy the composition. Check the overall appearance of your paper.

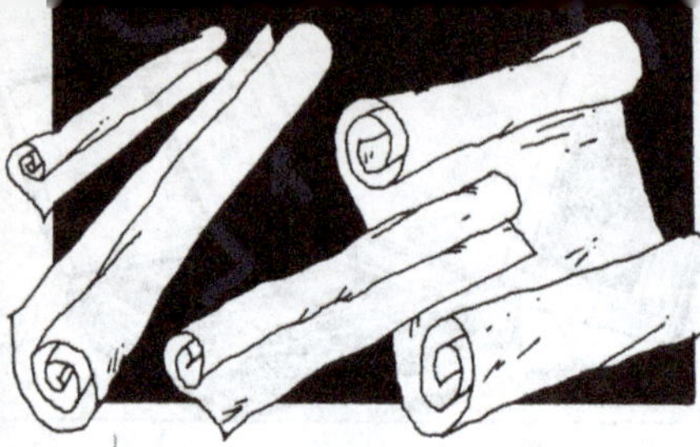

USING HANDWRITING: COMPOSITION

A composition usually contains two or more paragraphs. The first line of each paragraph is indented with a space as wide as a capital **O.**

Papermaking

The fine art of papermaking began in China. The first real paper was invented in China in A.D. 105 by Ts'ai Lun. He discovered that the inner bark of the mulberry tree could be broken into fibers and matted into sheets. The Chinese later found that fine paper could be made by pounding the fibers of old rags into sheets.

For hundreds of years, most paper was made from rags. Today, wood pulp is the principal raw material used to make paper. Even today, however, the finest paper, of the highest writing quality, is still made from rags.

The United States manufactures about 60 million tons of paper every year. In one year, each American uses more than 600 pounds of paper. How much paper do you think you use in a year?

Directions: Copy the composition.

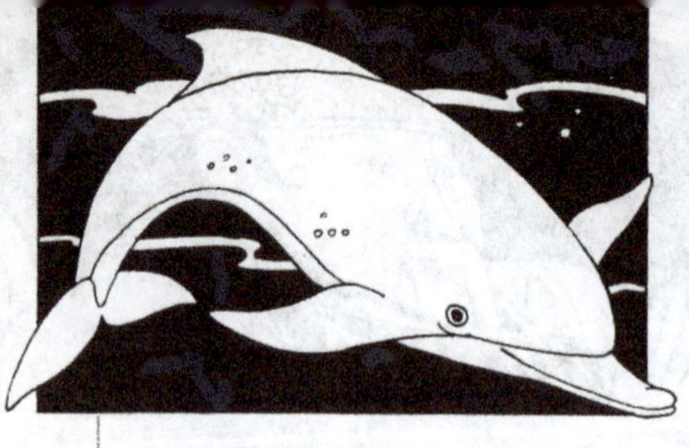

PROGRESS PAGES

Don Quixote, the hero of a novel by Miguel de Cervantes, fought injustice.

Xenophon, a Greek historian, wrote quite an exciting account of the Persian Wars.

Emily Bronte wrote about the moors of Yorkshire, England, where she was born.

Katherine Mansfield's stories were based on her childhood in New Zealand.

 Directions: Copy the sentences.

Edna St. Vincent Millay won a Pulitzer prize for her poetry in 1923.

Amy Lowell, Sara Teasdale, and Harriet Monroe were famous American poetesses.

Robert Frost, Louis Untermeyer, and Stephen Benet were famous American poets.

Sean O'Casey and James Stephens were talented Irish writers.

Directions: Copy the sentences.

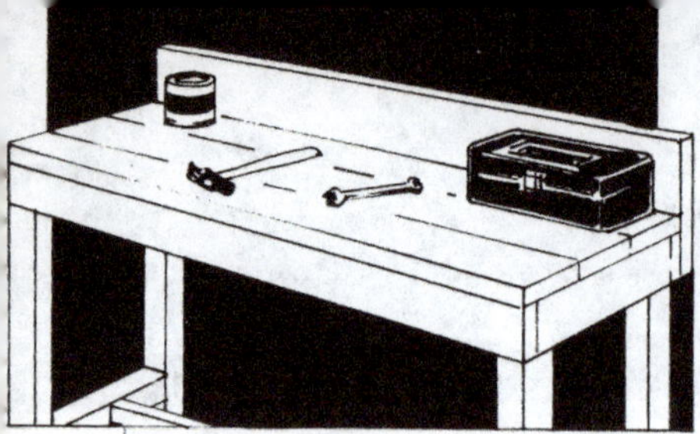

USING HANDWRITING: NUMBERED LIST

The items in this manuscript list are numbered. The numerals are lined up on the left, one under the other.

Avoiding Fire Hazards at Home

1. Check electrical wiring and replace wiring that is frayed or worn.
2. Check that electrical outlets are not overloaded by too many appliances.
3. Dispose of oil-soaked rags in covered containers.
4. Store flammable liquids, such as paint or gasoline, in tightly closed containers away from heat.

 Directions: Copy the list using manuscript handwriting.

USING HANDWRITING: WANT ADS

Abbreviations are often used in want ads to save space.

COMPUTER PROGRAMMER
Micro software co. looking for programmer with 3–5 yrs. exper. Tremendous growth oppty. Send resume to Dynamic Corp., 653 Woods St., Chicago, IL 60638

LIBRARIAN Call (312) 164-3579.
M.A. in Library Science and minimum two years library exper. req'd. Will entail some weekend and evening hrs. Must enjoy working w/young adults.

Directions: Copy the want ads using manuscript handwriting.

WRITING RHYTHMICALLY

Writing rhythmically will help you to write faster and more smoothly and easily.

1 e 1 e 1 e 1 e 1 e 1 1 1 1 1 eeeee

1-2 a 1-2 a 1-2 a 1-2 a 1-2 a 1-2 1-2 1-2 1-2 1-2 aaaaa

1-2 n 1-2 n 1-2 n 1-2 n 1-2 n 1-2 1-2 no 1-2 1-2 no

1-2 o 1-2 o 1-2 o 1-2 o 1-2 o 1-2-3 1-2 so 1-2-3 1-2 so

1-2 v 1-2 v 1-2 v 1-2 v 1-2 v 1-2 1-2 1-2 van 1-2 1-2 1-2 van

1-2 c 1-2 c 1-2 c 1-2 c 1-2 c 1-2 1-2 1-2 can 1-2 1-2 1-2-3 1 came

 Directions: Copy the letters and words as you count the strokes.

SIMPLIFYING LETTER FORMS FOR NAMES

Many people like to change their handwriting when they write their names in order to make their signatures more personal.

Timothy Timothy Timothy

Francisco Francisco Francisco

Marilyn Marilyn Marilyn

Kimberly Kimberly Kimberly

Violeta Violeta Violeta

Yoko Yoko Yoko

Directions: Copy the names using the capital letter form of your choice.

USING HANDWRITING: INVITATION

In this invitation, the heading, closing, and signature all begin in the middle of the line. The greeting begins at the left margin.

Heading
4302 Highland Road
Dallas, Texas 75221
March 6, 19__

Dear Luisa, Greeting

I am having a barbecue for the seventh grade class at my house on Friday, March 17, at 6 P.M. I hope you can come.

Closing Your friend,
Signature Jason Roberts

 Directions: Copy the invitation. Use today's date in the heading.

USING HANDWRITING: ADDRESSING AN ENVELOPE

On this envelope, the name and address of the person receiving the letter are written in the center of the envelope. The sender's name and address are written in the upper left corner.

Jason Roberts
4302 Highland Road
Dallas, Texas 75221

Miss Luisa Morales
6657 Citrus Drive
Dallas, Texas 75221

Directions: Copy the addresses.

USING HANDWRITING: PLAY

In a script for a play, each character's name is followed by a colon. A colon is made with two dots, one above the other.

Lost in the Forest

Setting: a forest at dusk

Ken: We're not heading in the right direction. I hate to admit it, but I'm afraid we're lost.

Nan: Don't worry. Clara will lead us back to the cabin.

Ken: We haven't seen Clara for more than an hour. She's lost, too.

Nan: Clara knows every inch of these woods. She'll come back.

Ken: Clara's nowhere in sight, and it's getting dark.

Nan: I hear a rustling noise.

Ken: Maybe it's a wild animal!

Nan: Maybe it's a tame one.

Ken: It's Clara!

Nan: Clara, you'll show us the way back, won't you?

Clara (wagging her tail): Arf! Arf!

 Directions: Copy the play.

PUNCTUATION MARKS

Your punctuation marks should be shaped like the models below and placed as shown in the sentences.

Have you read Johnny Tremain?

I've been here for twenty-five minutes.

Ms. Vega, our teacher, entered the room.

The meeting will be Friday, May 3.

"I'm not sure," said Gail, "if he's coming."

"What are you doing?" asked Akiko.

 Directions: Copy the sentences.

Sue needs thumbtacks, tape, and string.

"Halt!" said the guard at the museum.

"Haven't you heard the news, Carlos?"

Father said that dinner was ready.

"Hurrah!" cheered the crowd.

Is Dave's brother older than yours?

Directions: Copy the sentences.

USING HANDWRITING: BOOK REPORT

In a book report, the title and author of the book are usually written at the top of the first page. The title of a book is always underlined.

Title: *The Other Side of the Mountain*
Author: E. G. Valens

Jill Kinmont was a champion skier. She loved the speed and rhythm of the sport, the thrill of flying across snow like a bird, and the feel of her skis carving into deep snow. She learned to ski with grace, to race down steep slopes without fear, and to ski to win. Her dream was to ski in the Olympics.

Then, in a qualifying race, Jill crashed to earth at 40 miles per hour. Her fall left her completely paralyzed. She never stood up again.

After the tragic accident, Jill became a new kind of champion. She learned to use her body muscles in new ways. She earned a college degree and became a teacher of young children. Nothing could stop Jill. She learned to climb to the other side of the mountain.

 Directions: Copy the book report.

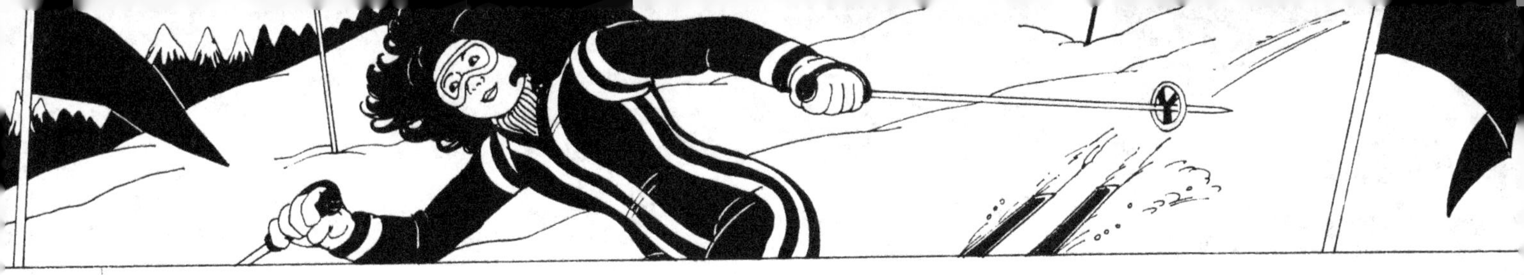

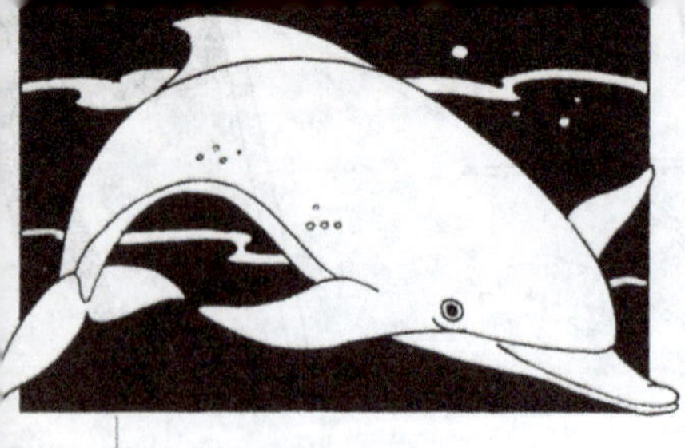

PROGRESS PAGES

Let's explore the world. In Africa we'll climb the lofty slopes of Mount Kilimanjaro, sail along the Zambezi River, and stand in awe before the majesty of Victoria Falls. We'll fly to Southeast Asia to visit the bustling city of Singapore, and on we'll go to the Far East to watch Chinese sampans cruise along Hong Kong's busy harbor. Perhaps we can arrive in Tokyo, the capital city of Japan, in time to enjoy a cherry blossom festival.

 Directions: Copy the paragraph.

On we'll go to North America. We'll trudge through the frozen tundra of the Yukon and admire the quaintness of historic Quebec. We'll drive across the United States from Boston to San Diego and stop to enjoy the sights of large cities like Atlanta, Georgia, and of small towns like Xenia, Ohio. And, finally, when we're safely back home, we'll dream of flying some day to Jupiter, to Mars, and beyond.

Directions: Copy the paragraph.

USING HANDWRITING: MEMO

A memo is a short, informal note. The memo below is written in the form of a letter.

October 1, 19__

Dear Students,

Are you enthusiastic? Do you like to work hard and have fun? Then I want you to work on the school year-book! Come to an orientation meeting tomorrow at 3 P.M. in the library.

Sincerely,
Dr. Wood

 Directions: Copy the memo using cursive handwriting. Use today's date in the heading.

USING HANDWRITING: PARAGRAPH

If a paragraph has a title, the title is usually centered on the first line with a blank line below.

Architects try to build strong, useful buildings that are beautiful to behold. But tastes change, and a building regarded as beautiful by one generation may be judged ugly by the next. Still, some buildings are marked by such strength and beauty that they stand out as master-pieces in any age. Such masterpieces include the graceful Parthenon of Athens, the imposing Colisseum of Rome and the stupendous pyramids of Egypt.

Directions: Write your own title. Then copy the paragraph using cursive handwriting.

FINAL TEST

The ancient Greeks dreamed of flying. So did Leonardo da Vinci. In 1903 the Wright Brothers of Dayton, OH flew just 120 feet. Quickly and quietly they flew, at Kitty Hawk, NC. Up rose their plane, opening the age of flight to valiant pioneers like Chuck Yeager, who broke the sound barrier in the amazing X-1. From there, humans exited Earth. Zooming into space went the proud rockets and spacecraft: Apollo, Jupiter, Redstone, Pioneer, and Mariner.

 Directions: Copy the paragraph.

HANDWRITING GUIDE SHEET

The Handwriting Guide Sheet is placed under your writing paper. It is used to check letters for correct slant and to check for uniform spacing between words.